Pat the pig's book

Pat the pig gets fit page 2
Pat the pig goes shopping
page 7
Pat the pig is ill page 12

HELEN MARRON
BOOKMARK
☎ 01213130256

Nelson

Pat the pig gets fit

"Pat, you are too fat.
You must run,"
said Ben.

"Pat, you are too fat.
You must skip,"
said Meg.

"Pat, you are too fat.
You must hop,"
said Deb.

"Pat, you are too fat.
You must bend,"
said Jip.

"Look at me,"
said Pat the pig.
"I am too fat."

Pat the pig goes shopping

"I will buy some
jam for Jip," said Pat the pig.
"I will see if it is good."
So he did.

"I will buy some
pop for Deb," said Pat the pig.
"I will see if it is good."
So he did.

"I will buy some
buns for Ben," said Pat the pig.
"I will see if they are good."
So he did.

"I will buy some
sweets for Sam," said Pat the pig.
"I will see if they are good."
So he did.

"I will go home now,"
said Pat the pig.
"I will go to bed."
And he did.

Pat the pig is ill

Pat the pig was sad.

He was in bed.

He had a cold.

Ben went to see Pat the pig.
"Here is a bone," said Ben.

Sam went to see Pat the pig.

"Here is a bun," said Sam.

"Thank you, thank you," said Pat the pig.